56 Mix Tips for the Small Recording Studio

Practical Techniques to Take Your Mixes to the Next Level

Copyright © 2014 Amos P. W. Clarke

All rights reserved.

Why I Wrote This Book

Before I wrote this book, if you asked me how many mixing techniques I regularly use I'd probably say around a half dozen. So it was a surprise to discover that actually it's more like 50 plus, being most of the techniques in this book. It was intriguing to discover how many of these techniques are so much a part of my every-day routine that they're almost invisible in my regular mixing routine and workflow.

Another main reason I wrote this book is that I felt a need for a book that simply gets down to business and gives readers solid and concise principles and instructions. There is an almost in-exhaustive supply of mixing books available that start right at the basics and cover off background, detail and lots of other peripheral information. If that's the kind of book you're looking for, then this book might not be for you. This book is the meat in the sandwich and gets right into an explanation of solid techniques right from the start. If you are a complete beginner you may find the use of jargon to be little confusing at times and although I've tried to keep this to a minimum, I've also included a glossary of terms at the end of the book in the event you need some clarification.

As an academic, lecturing at a tertiary level for over 15 years, I can't help but want to share my knowledge and experience – I guess it's in my blood. It's very satisfying for me to share my knowledge in the hope that I'm helping somebody else achieve their goals and potential. I've always been attracted to the idea of short-cutting my own learning by taking advantage of the experience and knowledge shared by someone who's been doing it. So I hope that's what you find this book to be for you; a short-cut to the meat in the sandwich.

Why You Should Read This Book

I spent over 10 years learning and fine-tuning these techniques and you can learn about them in around one to two hours (depending on your reading speed). That's probably a good enough reason alone for you to start reading right now.

What I can tell you with certainty, is that these techniques aren't some accumulation of content simply duplicated from the internet, other sources, or bogus ideas I dreamed up in an effort to pad out this book. The mix tips in this book are a combination of techniques I've discovered and adapted from my own research, communication with other mixing engineers, and general messing around and knob-twiddling in the studio. These mixing tips are all very effective and I use most of them (or variations), most of the time, on most of my own mixing productions. They can make a huge difference to the quality of your mixes if implemented with care – heck, you might find the missing ingredient that takes your mixes to the level. Over the years, some of them were 'ah-ha' moments for me and when I worked out how to really make them work in my music productions, they literally had me smiling for weeks – I hope it works this way for you too.

This book is designed so that you can turn to any page, find a mixing tip that you like and try it out. There is no up-front and brutal bombardment of the history and theory of mixing music. It reads more like a 'Don't Sweat the Small Stuff' of mixing music. There are 56 mixing tips and each one follows an almost identical format: a short explanation, why it's useful and how it works, and a 'Do It' section showing you how to implement the technique into your mix. I personally love reading books like this that simply get down to business without the fluff. However, this book requires at least some basic understanding of mixing music to give you the most value. You don't need to read the book in any set order of chapters since there are none. Simply flick through it, see what grabs your attention, and dig in! For your convenience, the chapters in the contents list are all hyper-linked.

Lastly, please note that any suggestion or recommendation of plugins I make is to assist in helping you understand and apply the technique. I am not affiliated or connected with any plugin companies and I make no money if you buy a plugin suggested by me.

So without holding you up any further, I sincerely hope you get lots out of this and it helps you take your own mixing to the next level.

Sincerely

Amos Clarke

Contents

Why I Wrote This Book
Why You Should Read This Book
Contents
01 Fat Tracks
02 Big Long Kick
03 Snappy Snare
04 Mono the Low End
05 Ambient Tracks
06 Macro-Compression
07 Reverse It
08 Filter the Lows
09 Mutant
10 Haas Delays
11 Complementary EQ
12 Stereo Spread
13 Drum Thickener
14 Mix Thickener
15 Crispy Toms
16 Gated Drums
17 Re-amp It
18 EQ Your Verb
19 Analyze It
20 Mid and Sides
21 Low Mono Listening
22 Roomy Drums
23 Comb Filtering

56 Mix Tips for the Small Recording Studio

24 LCR Panning

25 Macro-EQ

26 Saturate It

27 Mix Focus

28 Mud, Box and Honk

29 Vocal Clarity

30 Big Tune-Up

31 Parallel Mix Compression

32 Stop Trying So Hard

33 Mix Interest

34 Guitar Amp Sims

35 Width, Depth and Height

36 Add Some Air

37 Filter the Highs

38 RMS/Peak Compression

39 Correction vs Character: Equalisation

40 Correction vs Character: Compression

41 Freaky Filters

42 Re-pitch it

43 Chorus Character

44 Limitation = Innovation

45 Ping Pong Delays

46 Phonc It In

47 Arrangement Transitions

48 Satellite Monitoring

49 Distort It

50 Compression Side-chain

51 Snare Thump

52 Kick Thump

53 Top & Tails

54 Transient & Sustain

55 Consistent Hits

56 Vocal Creativity

Glossary

Thanks

Other Books by Amos Clarke

About The Author

01
Fat Tracks

Duplicate existing tracks, add FX and mix back in with the original for fatness, fullness, and character

This technique works great on just about everything, but I use it mostly on main vocals, bass, kick and snare. It's a great way to add a fullness character to your track while emphasizing particular frequency zones. It is a very similar effect to parallel compression because the processing involves fairly heavy compression or limiting and blending back in to your mix. The technique requires you to duplicate an existing track, add treatment, and then mix it back in with your original track. Treatment primarily involves compression and equalisation. Adding the treatment on a duplicated track (instead of on the original track) has the advantage of making it easier to control the blend of the effect during mixing by a simple fader adjustment, rather than having to open the plugin to change settings.

Do It: Example using electric bass track

1. While retaining the original track, duplicate the entire bass track and apply the following treatment on the duplicated track. Do not make any adjustments to the original track other than general EQ or compression that you may have done anyway.

2. Apply a gentle sloped high pass filter at around 500 Hz (or to taste) and a low pass filter at around 5 kHz to control the high frequencies and harshness that can result.

3. Apply heavy limiting with around 10 dB of gain reduction.

4. Mix this back in to the original bass track to get a nice mid-range growl

Amos Clarke

with some high end clarity. You can also add saturation (distortion) for more bite.

02

Big Long Kick

Get a big, full-bodied kick drum sound - variation on the 'fat track' technique

The kick drum forms an important part of the rhythm section in most songs. In dense rock mixes for example (dense being when there are many heavily compressed elements playing simultaneously), the key to getting any percussive element to stand out without simply raising the level is to enhance the initial transient and the sustain. The transient is the initial peak at the front of the waveform and enhancing this creates an emphasis that allows the element (such as a kick or snare drum) to 'poke' out in the mix. The reason for adding sustain to percussive elements is because these short bursts of audio (e.g. a kick drum) can lose definition in a dense mix due to frequency masking. Increasing the sustain is based on the principle that the longer the duration of an element, the easier it is to hear it. When we combine transient and sustain processing, we have a very effective technique to make percussive sounds stand out in any mix.

Do It:

1. Create a duplicate track of the original kick drum track and apply the following processing to the duplicated track. Do not apply any of the processing to your original track for this effect.

2. On the duplicated track, firstly apply gating to remove as much other drum bleed as possible so that you have, if possible, only the kick drum audible.

3. Now apply heavy compression or limiting of around 10 dB gain reduction. Use a fast or slow attack depending on whether you want to retain the initial transient.

Amos Clarke

4. Add some mild saturation (distortion) to add bite – go easy on the level as a little goes a long way.

5. Lastly, add a mono reverb to provide further sustain. It's important to keep the reverb **mono** to avoid placing extreme low frequencies into the left and right sides of your mix (which happens if you use a stereo reverb). If necessary, apply a little high pass filtering to the reverb to remove any low frequencies that may be too dominant.

6. You can now blend the effect of this duplicated track in with your original kick by simply adjusting the fader level.

Amos Clarke

03

Snappy Snare

Get punch, snap and excellent clarity for snare drums in dense mixes

This technique involves manipulating the initial transient at the start of the waveform. The principle behind why this technique is effect is outlined in mix tip '02'. I will reiterate that it is a very effective way to add clarity and definition to your snare drum in dense mixes. In less dense mixes, it's a very useful technique for adding a little articulation and presence. It is important not to over-do this effect as it can sound bad if abused. Additionally, you can use combinations of this technique, such as only applying transient treatment and ignoring sustain treatment. Or you can do it the other way around, or apply both. However you use it, this technique will prove a fantastic way to add character to your snare drum. There are plugins designed to do this, such as the SPL Transient Designer or the Stillwell Audio's Transient Monster. That's the easy way to do it and involves simply adding such a plugin to your plugin chain. If you don't have access to one of these specialist plugins, then you can achieve the same effect using any standard compressor with manual attack, release, and threshold settings. See below for how to achieve this using a standard compressor.

Do It: Using a standard compressor

If you are applying this effect with a specialist plugin, such as the SPL Transient Designer, then the process is as simple as inserting the plugin on your original snare track and adjusting to taste.

1. Duplicate the original snare track and apply the following treatment (retain the original track).

2. Apply gating to remove all other drum bleed except for the snare hits.

Amos Clarke

3. Using a compressor, set the attack to approximately 20 ms, release to around 100 ms, and ratio to 10:1.

4. Adjust the threshold by ear, to achieve a very obvious and powerful 'thwack'. You will need to lower the threshold significantly to achieve this and it will sound a bit horrible in isolation. Make level adjustments to avoid serious clipping if necessary.

5. If required, add a limiter afterwards to tame the peaks – but use extreme care as too much limiting will negate the effect.

6. Mix back in with the original snare track to achieve a vibrant snap to your snare drum.

Amos Clarke

04

Mono the Low End

Get clarity and definition with the low end of your mix

One way to get clarity in your overall mix is to have good low-end definition. In other words, a clear, non-muddy, and defined, low frequency range. While a defined low end is as much to do about correct equalisation and balancing, 'mono-ing' the low frequencies on your overall mix can make a big difference in creating a clarity that creates a defined bass and the kick drum. Mid-range instruments are often culprits here, such as electric guitars with too much low frequency content. If this is the case, then you would need to apply independent high pass filtering to all offending guitars to remove these low frequencies, as mono-ing the mix's low end simply blends this 'mud' with your kick and bass.

The technique involves inserting a specialist plugin that turns your stereo mix into mono from a certain frequency and below. This effectively removes low frequencies from the left and right sides of your mix by turning them to mono from the chosen frequency. You can select and tune this frequency to taste. Note that this operation would usually be done near the end of your mix as a fine-tuning operation.

Some available plugins that will do this are:

+ Izotope Ozone (www.izotope.com)
+ Brainworx Control-V2 (www.brainworx.com)

Do It

1. Insert plugin on your master buss.

2. Using the plugin, select the frequency from which frequency and below,

Amos Clarke

your mix will become mono – I usually start with around 125 Hz and adjust to taste.

3. Check your mix against a reference song to help you fine-tune the frequency point.

05

Ambient Tracks

Add depth and fullness to your overall mix by adding low-level elements with delay-based effects

This technique involves using stereo instrumental elements that are rich in sustain and low in initial transient peaks. It works well to have these elements playing at a very low volume as the intention is not to draw attention to themselves, but rather produce a reinforcing effect to the mix. By placing these elements at strategic places in your mix, you can create an effective 'thickening' and added interest. We need to avoid the transients when selecting the sounds as transient-rich audio material tends to draw attention to itself, and that's not what we want here. These elements can add a wonderful 'thickening' effect to your mix when added in at low levels, and a nice depth from the addition of spacious reverb effects. This effect can work very well with 'mid-range' rich elements such as those noted in the examples below.

Examples:

+ String ensembles
+ Sustained one-hit guitar and keyboard chords
+ Synth samples
+ Vocal ensembles

Do It

1. Select a stereo ambient element such as a keyboard sample and ensure it has its own track.

2. Add an EQ or filtering plugin and tune the low and high end with HPF and LPF's so that unwanted extreme low and high frequencies are removed.

Amos Clarke

You could start with HPF @ 150 Hz and LPF @ 5 kHz.

3. Add a medium to large stereo reverb. In some cases you will need to apply further filtering to reduce or remove low and high frequency reverb artifacts.

4. Mix back in to the song at a low level. I usually work on the basis of raising the level until I can just hear it, then backing it off a couple of dB.

06

Macro-Compression

Apply compression quickly and effectively to achieve a fuller sound to groups of instruments in your mix

Save time by applying compression treatment on groups of tracks before individual tracks. The reason this is a time-saver is because you are applying compression on a group that may have many tracks, rather than on those individual tracks themselves. It does require more care with the setting of the compressor and the elements that are routed to that group. For example, if you were applying compression to a group of rhythm guitars, you need to ensure that there are no transient-rich tracks that are at a high volume as these tracks will tend to activate the compressor, thereby applying compression to the entire group.
To apply this technique, route similar sounding instruments to stereo group busses in your mix session, then apply compression to the group. The aim is to create a fuller sound to these instruments by applying gentle compression or limiting.

This works effectively with the following:

+ Foundation elements: drums and bass
+ Mid-range instruments: guitars and keyboards
+ Ambient elements: string ensembles, vocal ensembles

Do it: Example using mid-range instruments in a mix

1. Create a stereo buss track and name it 'G.Inst'. This is your stereo group track for all instruments.

2. Route all keyboards, electric, and acoustic guitars to this group (exclude solo instruments, such as a lead guitar).

3. Apply your compression plugin to the 'G.Inst' group and aim for 3-5 dB of gain reduction - adjust attack, release and threshold to taste.

Amos Clarke

07

Reverse It

Create character and uniqueness in the mix by adding reversed elements into your mix

This technique involves rendering short sections of an element in your mix, reversing it, and adding it back into the mix at different sections of your song for extra character. I often use this as a way to 'thicken' a chorus section (mixed in at very low level). It is also an effective way of creating a transition between a verse and chorus, or chorus/solo, or chorus/verse. For these types of transitions creating a fade-in on the rendered audio clip works well. It is also very effective as a way to emphasize other parts within a section of the song by mixing in at a low level. Be careful when using this technique on any element with a strong melody or chords as these may clash harmonically with the instrumentation playing in that section.

Here are a few of the elements that can work well this technique:

+ Individual drum hits, like kick and snare
+ Drum room mic
+ Rhythm guitars
+ Backing vocals
+ Entire song

Do it: example using electric guitars

1. Select a short (couple of bars) section of guitars anywhere that sounds interesting and render this out to a stereo file.

2. Open the file in an editor and reverse it so it plays backwards. Create a very short fade in/out to avoid clicks at the start and end of the audio.

Amos Clarke

4. In your multi-track session, create a track solely for adding your 'reversed' audio renders and add your new audio where necessary. You may find it useful to add delay effect plugins and limiting to tame the dynamics and sculpt the frequency range. HPF and LPF are almost always required to control the amount of low and high frequencies introduced back into the mix. As stated earlier, if inserting at a transition between two sections, a fade-in from nothing can be effective. If using at other parts of the song, adjust your level carefully so that you achieve a tasteful blend that enhances the music in that section – usually this works well later in a song when trying to increase the energy dynamic in the song.

5. Adjust the level to suit. Once again, having the effect on its own channel makes for easy level balancing during mixing.

08

Filter the Lows

Add clarity to your mix by removing unwanted low frequencies from your tracks

This technique involves filtering out the low frequencies on almost every track to add definition to the 'low end' of your mix. The reason is that the more tracks in your session, the more likely you will have a build-up of low frequency content, which will start to 'muddy up' the low end of your mix. It's generally not necessary to apply high pass filtering to bass instruments, such as kick drum and bass guitar, but every other element should generally have the low end rolled off. The key here is to get the knee of the roll-off at the right frequency so you don't remove too much or too little. Using this technique will be very effective in helping create a defined low end in your overall mix. It's good practice to have a LPF (low pass filter) as the first plugin on every track to achieve this.

Examples of how this works with different instruments (these can vary depending on the material):

+ Kick drum and electric bass: HPF @ +/- 50 Hz
+ Drum Over-heads: +/- 150 Hz
+ Electric guitar: HPF @ +/- 125 Hz
+ Backing vocal (telephone style): HPF @ +/- 500 Hz

Do It

1. Add a HPF plugin as the first plugin on all tracks. This includes the low frequency tracks like kick drum and bass guitar as sometimes they will require removal of very low frequency rumble.

Amos Clarke

2. Solo the track and slowly adjust the frequency roll-off until you hear the bass frequencies begin to disappear, then back it off slightly. The goal here is to remove frequencies that are not contributing to the mix.

3. Now play the entire song and adjust the frequency roll-off again. The aim here is to avoid clashes with other low frequency instruments.

4. Try doing this technique in groups. For example, route all your electric guitars to a stereo group channel and insert the HPF on the group, rather than adding a HPF plugin to every guitar track.

Amos Clarke

09

Mutant

Clean up your entire mix by muting clashing and distracting mix elements

This is the easiest and most effective technique I know to clean up a mix. I often get mixes where there is simply too much instrumentation playing simultaneously at different points in the song. This can cause mushy and confusing sounding mixes that lack definition because of frequency masking and competing lead elements. To many elements playing at the same time can create ear fatigue and confusion for the listener due to loss of focus (such as a lead vocal and strong guitar melody playing together). The issue of frequency masking is apparent when two similar sounding elements are playing, and both become undefined. A common example is with mid-range elements such as vocals, electric guitars, and keyboards (organs). The aim is to mute the offending elements without upsetting the vibe and direction of the song. Sometimes it can be tough to decide which element to mute. However, carefully considered muting is a wonderfully effective way to create a cleaner and clearer mix.

Do it

1. When your mix is well advanced, listen carefully to all the elements playing and listen for clashing elements, such as lead elements fighting and loss of clarity of an instrument.

2. Identify elements that are causing problems and experiment by muting them to see if they create more clarity and definition in the mix. Often, muting will involve simply muting a note or two, or consecutive bars.

3. Decide on your final mutes and remove or automate mutes during the mix.

Amos Clarke

It's worthwhile to not delete the material in case your band/client decides that you have removed important elements from the mix. This is why muting is such a great and easy technique: what's muted can simply be un-muted.

Amos Clarke

10

Haas Delays

Create a realistic sense of space to hard-panned mid-range mono instruments by adding very short delays

Haas delays are very short delays that are not perceived by the ear to be a separate occurrence of the original sound. They can however, be used to create an obvious ambience and space around an element that is just enough to 'put some air around it' without creating an obvious delay or reverb effect. Using almost any delay plugin, you can create a sense of real space to a mono instrument by using delay settings of 0.1 ms to 20 ms. This is a very effective technique to employ if you use LCR panning because elements which are panned hard left or right miss a sense of realism, particularly on headphones because they can only be heard in one side of the headset. By adding a short delay and panning this to the opposite side, a real sense of 'dry' space is added around that element.

Do It: Example using acoustic guitar

1. Using a single acoustic guitar track recorded in mono, pan this track 100% left.

2. Duplicate this track and add a delay plugin, setting the delay to 20 ms. Ensure there is no 'dry' signal present. Another alternative would be simply to create a 'send' to a an FX buss with your short delay on it and pan this to 50% right as stated in step 3).

3. Pan the duplicated track 50% right and lower the level.

4. You should now have achieved a sense of real space around the instrument without using reverb or an obvious delay. The effect can be adjusted simply

Amos Clarke

by raising or lowering the fader of the duplicated track.

Note: *You could also achieve this by using a 'send' to a delay effect.*

11

Complementary EQ

Create width and definition between same sounding instruments using this equalisation technique

This technique involves making complementary EQ adjustments to similar sounding instruments and elements which are on opposing tracks and works best using a parametric EQ because you need the ability to boost and cut certain frequency nodes with some precision. It works by carefully selecting 2-3 EQ nodes for each track, then making opposite EQ adjustments at the same frequency nodes on the opposite track. It is an and effective way to add subtle definition same instruments that are panned both left and right because the opposing adjustments to the frequencies create minute differences that help the ear to differentiate, therefore adding clarity to the mix. The technique is also effective on elements that have a much closer panning (such as panned 10% left and 10% right) and even on elements that have centred panning.

Examples of instruments/elements for this technique:

+ Electric guitars
+ Acoustic guitars
+ Keyboards
+ Backing vocals

Do It: example using electric guitars

1. Firstly, select and work on two tracks simultaneously. Use two guitars that were recorded with the same or similar settings. It is worthwhile first up, to have a careful listen to each guitar track before applying the following steps to ensure you don't boost harsh or problem frequencies. These can be bass frequencies, very high frequencies that can add brittleness, and harsh

Amos Clarke

frequencies around the 2 – 3 kHz range. The following frequencies are suggestions only.

2. Left electric guitar track: <u>boost</u> 3 dB @ 125 Hz, <u>cut</u> 3 dB @ 800 Hz, <u>boost</u> 1.5 dB @ 4 kHz.

3. Right electric guitar track: <u>cut</u> 3 dB @ 125 Hz, <u>boost</u> 3 dB @ 800 Hz, <u>cut</u> 1.5 dB @ 4 kHz.

4. Once you have made these adjustments, scrutinize your entire mix to ensure you haven't created problematic frequency masking with other mix elements from the EQ boosts you just applied.

Note: *Ensure your boosts use a 'wide' bell curve and your cuts use a narrower bell curve and try different frequencies to taste.*

Amos Clarke

12
Stereo Spread

Create width to mix elements – great for sparse mixes or adding character to lead elements

This technique simply involves applying a small amount of stereo spread to a mono mix element to give it more width in the overall mix-scape. It also works great when the song has only a few instruments because it can increase the apparent width of an instrument to provide a fuller sounding mix. Be careful not to add too much as a little goes a long way and you can cause phase cancellation problems that may cause the song to lose clarity when played in mono. When applying the effect, your aim is to create a mild enhancement to the element so it sounds slightly 'widened' in the mix. This technique is very effective if you want to give more apparent spread to your mix while still keeping it relatively dry sounding, without resorting to stereo reverbs.

It can work great on:

+ Lead vocals
+ Lead guitar
+ Bass (be careful as this can add bass to the sides of the mix)

Do It:

1. Apply a 'stereo spread' plugin to the track that you want to widen. Apply small amounts as too much can cause phasing problems.

2. Regularly check the results with the entire mix playing and listen in mono to check for phase cancellation.

Amos Clarke

Note: *There are free plugins that will do the job nicely. I use Voxengo 'Stereo Touch, free from www.voxengo.com.*

Amos Clarke

13

Drum Thickener

Beef up your drums to create a more punchy and solid sounding performance

This is a technique I love and use on almost every mix. It involves sending all drum tracks to a stereo drum group track and applying parallel compression to the group. Parallel compression allows you to retain the original drum dynamics while mixing in a heavily compressed version of the drums. The result: a drum track that still retains the original dynamics, but with a thicker, beefier character. Use a plugin compressor that has a wet/dry mix knob so that you have control over how much compression you dial in. Be careful with the attack and release settings on your compressor as this can significantly affect the 'flavour' of the parallel compression. For example, setting the attack at around 20 – 30 ms will allow drum transients through the compressor and will tend to add more punch and snap to the compressed signal, whereas setting a fast attack will all but eliminate these transients. The best thing is to try it out and see what you like. Similarly, care taken with the release setting will yield other different flavours. For example, long release times can create a more limiting effect, where shorter release times can cause 'pumping'. Pumping is usually an effect you want to avoid but it may well be a creative solution for your song.

Do It:

1. Route all drum tracks to a stereo drum group channel.

2. Apply a compressor plugin. Set the compressor to give around 10 dB+ gain reduction. Set slow attacks to allow drum transients through, or fast attacks to remove these peaks and create a different character. It will sound bad to start with because you are applying heavy compression to your drums

Amos Clarke

– but hang in there. Adjust attack and release settings so that there is an even balance of instruments.

3. Dial back the wet/dry knob so that you are now only adding in around +/- 15% of this compressed signal. Adjust to taste.

Note: *Some care is required with the setting of attack and release times on the compressor as the wrong settings can cause pumping and accentuate elements that don't sound good. It's not fun to have hi-hats blasting through your drum mix.*

Amos Clarke

14

Mix Thickener

Create a thicker, denser flavour to your mix by adding background noise

This method is great for adding an undefined 'thickening' to a musical section – in the studio we tend to use the term 'corn flour'. It can also work well used as a transition from a verse to a chorus, chorus to solo, chorus back to verse, and so on. The technique involves adding ambient sound effects at strategic points in your mix. It's a good idea to select audio material that has little or no obvious transients that may stick out in the mix. I personally use this technique mostly as 'corn flour' to create a fuller sound in sections of a song requiring a denser vibe, such as a chorus or outro. This is useful because it helps in creating overall song dynamics by thickening the important sections of the song, then removing it to create a sparser vibe in the verses. Once again, don't overdo this effect and aim to keep the level of the audio at a lower level – it wants to be there, but not making a statement.

Suggestions of different types of background sounds that can work well:

+ Recorded ambient street/traffic/conversational noise
+ Reversed background vocals, drums, or guitars rendered from your song
+ Ambient synth samples

Do It:

1. Select any mono or stereo tracks as suggested above and add to a new track in your mix session. Try different sections to locate the material, such as in choruses, or only in a bridge.

Amos Clarke

2. Try adding reverb, delays, and saturation effects.

3. Mix in at low level to taste.

15

Crispy Toms

Create cleaner sounding toms by removing ambient drum noise

If you want to have clean, crisp sounding drums then you'll need to spend time removing ambient drum noise from tracks. This technique focuses on muting/removing entire sections of bleed from your tom tracks. In other words, you remove everything that isn't a tom. I use this method because I get better results than relying on gating, which can be wrongly triggered by snare and kick drum bleed on the tom track.

Do It:

1. After selecting the tom track, listen carefully to find all locations of the tom hits throughout the song.

2. 'Snip' and mute the sections where not toms are playing. Be accurate with your snip locations to avoid other unnecessary drum sounds remaining.

3. Listen for cymbal hits that may coincide with the tom hits. For each of these cymbal/tom hits, create a hard edit using a LPF to roll off the top end and reduce the cymbal sound – be careful not to dull the tom too much. See my note below for an alternative option if this is unsuccessful.

4. Create a short fade out if needed to give the tom a natural decay.

Note: *It's not uncommon to run up against problems when editing, where you might have a hi-hat or cymbal hit with the tom, making it almost impossible to remove the cymbal hit. In this case, try swapping out the offending hit with a clean tom hit from another part of the track.*

Amos Clarke

16

Gated Drums

Create cleaner, more distinct drums by gating ambient drum noise

This technique involves using a gate to remove unnecessary drum bleed from drum tracks to achieve cleaner sounding tracks. The goal here is to apply a gate to all drum tracks in an attempt to provide a clean and tight sounding drum kit and typically <u>excludes</u> gating overhead and room drum mics as we want to retain all the audio captured from these mic's. It's important to take time with the tuning of the gate plugin as incorrect tuning can remove drum hits. Listen to your entire tracks in solo when gating and tune them individually for each different drum.

Common drum tracks requiring gating:

+ Kick drum track
+ Snare drum track
+ Tom tracks
+ Other percussion like shakers, tambourines etc.

Do It: Example using kick drum track

1. Insert a gate plugin as the first instance in your plugin chain.

2. Solo and play the kick drum track while tuning the gate so that you remove all other ambient drum noise except for the kick drum.

3. When tuning, start with the gate threshold level first and use a very fast attack. Adjust the 'fade' or 'decay' so that the kick drum doesn't stop too abruptly. Some gates have a tuning feature which allows for simpler tuning.

Amos Clarke

17

Re-amp It

Breathe life and character into existing recorded tracks by re-processing with external hardware

Re-amping is a great technique to breathe new life into existing recorded tracks. Re-amping involves sending an output of your original recording into an external piece of hardware which will alter the tone. This 're-amped' signal is then re-recorded back into your DAW session to a separate track and can be mixed in with the original or simply replace it.

Examples of re-amping:

+ A clean electric guitar tone is recorded. The recorded track is then re-amped by sending to a guitar amp which is mic'd up and re-recorded. The new re-amped track is then mixed in with the original guitar recording.
+ A main vocal is recorded clean. This track is then re-amped through an external hardware compressor and re-recorded. The heavily compressed track is then mixed back in at a low level to provide a more solid and consistent sounding performance to the vocal.
+ A snare drum is fed out to a guitar foot pedal to give a trashy sustain effect. It is then re-mixed back in with the original snare drum to provide a bigger, thicker sounding snare drum for a rock song.

Do It: Example using a clean electric guitar

1. Check your interface has outputs that enable you to send a single track to one of the outputs.

2. Send the output of the clean guitar track to a 're-amp box', then into the instrument input of the guitar amplifier and mic up the amplifier.

Amos Clarke

3. Record the mic'd amplifier into your session.

Note: *some care is required to ensure that your re-amped track is time-aligned to the original track to avoid phasing.*

18

EQ Your Verb

Improve the tonality and character of your reverb by applying EQ treatment

This technique involves applying an EQ plugin after your reverb in your plugin chain. It's worthwhile EQing your reverbs because there's often a need to reduce or remove high and low frequencies which can become dominant in the mix. Depending on the quality of your reverb plugin, they can develop nasty mid frequency resonances and these can also be removed by a narrow bell curve cut with a parametric EQ. When applying reverb effects, it's good practice to create 'sends' from your recorded tracks to a separate channel that has the reverb. However, some reverb plugins have EQ control built in, but if yours doesn't or you simply want to place a high quality EQ on your reverb, this is how to do it.

Do It:

1. Create a reverb send channel: create a new stereo or mono channel.

2. Insert your selected reverb plugin, followed by an EQ plugin.

3. Create a send from your instrument track: Assuming your DAW has a 'send' option, designate a send output to the 'reverb send channel'.

4. Make EQ adjustments while soloing the track and with the entire song mix playing. When soloing, listen for boomy low frequencies, and high frequencies such as sibilance, clicking and ringing and use HPF and LPFs to roll-off these frequencies. Listen for harsh mid frequencies, particularly around the 2 – 3 kHz region.

Amos Clarke

19

Analyze It

Keep a visual reference as your mix progresses

This technique requires you to regularly check your mix with a spectrum analyzer while mixing by inserting a suitable plugin as the final instance in your master buss plugin chain. While it's most important to trust your ears and compare to a reference song, it becomes even more valuable if your studio listening environment is sub-optimal. Remember that how your mix sounds is more important than how it looks, so trust your ears. If you do fall into the category of a not-so-good listening environment, simply play your mix back on multiple systems and compare it to similar pro mixes. A good sounding mix usually shows as a fairly consistent spectrum, however this does depend on the resolution and speed of your analyzer plugin – read the instructions to set it up optimally for your needs.

Key things to check on the spectrum analyzer:

+ Overall frequency extension (where the low end and high end frequencies roll off)
+ Frequency extension on the 'mid' and 'side' channels
+ Loudness in both peak and RMS modes
+ Check how your reference song looks on the analyzer compared to your own mix

Do It:

1. For overall frequency extension, aim for a moderate roll off of low frequencies at approximately 100 Hz, and a slow taper of high frequencies at around 5 kHz.

Amos Clarke

2. Check the frequency extension of 'mid' and 'side' channels and compare to your reference song.

3. Ensure peak levels do not exceed -3 dB FS if you are creating a final mix for mastering.

Amos Clarke

20

Mid and Sides

Get clear and even dispersion of frequencies in your mixes by controlling the mid and side elements in the mix

Listen to the 'mid' and 'side' channels of any professional mix and you'll notice common characteristics about the placement of mix elements and the dispersion of frequencies. Understanding how the pro's structure the mid/sides of their mixes can help you structure great mixes to. You need to use a spectrum analyzer with a mid/side function, like Voxengo Span (www.voxengo.com). Refer to '19 Analyze It' for more information about mid/side.

Revealing things I discovered during my investigation of many pro mixes over the years:

+ The punchiest mixes have kick, bass and snare drum almost entirely in the mid channel.

+ Mixes with the clearest low end have no low bass elements in the side channel and commonly tend to roll off at around 100 Hz.

+ Side channels with a mildly elevated high frequency extension seem to sound 'wider'.

+ Nicely compressed mixes do not seem to 'bounce around' much in the side channels.

Do It:

1. Insert a spectrum analyzer plugin on your master buss. Use a plugin that

Amos Clarke

has the ability to show the 'mid' and the 'side' frequency content separately.

2. Ensure your mix session includes a reference song on a separate track.

3. Select the 'mid' frequency display option on the analyzer plugin. Play your own mix then revert to the reference song, all the while comparing how the spectrum reacts.

4. Repeat step 2 with the 'sides' selected.

5. Use this comparison and measurement technique to help you fine-tune your mix balance. If you need to make corrections to your mix, make appropriate level or EQ adjustments on the tracks, rather than adding an EQ plugin on the master buss.

Amos Clarke

21

Low Mono Listening

Monitor to your mixes in mono at low level to reveal just how clear your mixes really are

This technique involves listening in mono on a single bandwidth limited speaker. Frequency masking becomes much more apparent when listening in mono and phase cancellations become obvious by a drop in level of a particular mix element. When we reduce frequency masking in our mixes, our mixes take on transparency and definition. It's important to note that listening on a small speaker such as those mentioned below will reduce the bass and high frequency content on the mix, so don't be tempted to boost the low and high frequencies of your mix. Your goal is to listen for overall mix clarity and generally aim for level or panning adjustments to improve the mix. To combat the reduced low and high frequency performance of smaller speakers, it's good practice to A-B your mix with your reference song so that you can get a good idea of how a professionally produced song sounds on the smaller monitor.

Another important point to be aware of is that our ears' sensitivity to across the full frequency range changes relative to the loudness. Even when listening on full range monitors, at high and low volumes the perceived frequency spectrum of your mix will vary so be aware of this. For example, when listening at different volumes you might experience variations in the level of the low end of your mix, leading you to make possible unnecessary EQ adjustments. Once again, the key is to 'reset' your ears by comparing to a reference song regularly while listening at low levels in mono. It's also a good idea to settle on one volume level and don't adjust it. To find out more, research Fletcher Munson's Equal Loudness Contours.

In days-gone-by, it was common to use a single Auratone for this technique, but good substitutes are:

Amos Clarke

+ Avantone Mix Cubes
+ Behringer C50A Studio Monitor

Do It:

1. Ensure your mix output is actually playing in mono – don't just send one side of your mix to this speaker.

2. Guidelines for listening:
a) Listen at low levels
b) Check for definition between the different elements
c) Check for clarity of the lead vocals
d) Listen for level drops on elements – there may be a phase cancellation issue in the mix
e) Listen to a reference song and continue A-Bing between this and your own mix for comparisons

Note: *Instruments panned to the centre will be emphasized – compare with your reference song*

Amos Clarke

22

Roomy Drums

Add fullness to your drum sound by adding a pseudo 'drum room mic'

Having a 'room' track is essential to adding fullness, ambience and bringing life to a drum kit. The 'room' track is simply a mic or pair of mic's placed away from the drum kit in a part of the room that picks up the recording of the room ambience. If you don't have a 'room' mic, then this technique shows you how to get fairly close to one. Once you understand the characteristics of how a room mic sounds, it becomes easier to create a 'faux' room mic track.

Characteristics of a room mic are typically:

+ Noticeable reverb
+ Room 'tone' such as a fuller low end or accentuated mid frequencies
+ Less high frequency content
+ All drums sounding more balanced
+ A reduction of transients

Do It:

1. Select one of your drum overhead tracks and copy this to another track in your DAW session.

2. Heavily compress or limit this 'room' track to taste, but avoid distortion.

3. Using the 'shelving filter' on your EQ, roll off some of the high frequencies slightly.

4. Add a reverb plugin and select a medium room.

Amos Clarke

5. Mix this in with your drum kit at a low to medium level depending on the character you're after.

Note: *Listen to real drum 'room' mics to help getter better understanding of what a real drum room mic recording can sound like.*

23

Comb Filtering

Add a unique character to make elements stand out in the mix

This is a great technique to use when EQ, compression or simply raising the volume doesn't provide the required definition in the mix. Comb filtering is an effective way to change the character of an element, thereby providing more clarity in the mix, however it does require some care as too much of this effect can cause the element to drop out when the mix is collapsed to mono. The application involves using a simple delay plugin and mixing a very short delayed signal with the original. The key thing is to apply the effect carefully and checking the result with your mix collapsed to mono.

Do It:

1. Select your individual track and add a delay plugin of any type. It's best to insert this rather than creating a send to a delay buss.

2. Ensure that all repeating and ping-pong effects are turned off and that the panning of the delay is set exactly the same as the original track pan position.

3. Select a delay time of anywhere between 0.1 ms through to 10 ms. Apply the effect sparingly and listen in the context of the entire mix.

Amos Clarke

24

LCR Panning

Create wide, clear, and defined mixes and save time while you do it

LCR panning is simply an abbreviation for 'Left, Centre, Right' and relates to the pan positions of elements in your mix. The technique primarily involves choosing one of these three panning positions for all of your instruments/mix elements. I love and use this technique on almost every mix I do because it massively speeds up my workflow (less decisions to make) and achieves wider, clearer sounding mixes with more separation. It often requires some augmentation for single elements (that are not lead effects) that are panned hard left or right as they can sound a little un-natural, particularly in headphones. This is because in a real world listening environment, sound sources are heard with both our ears, not just one. Luckily there is an easy and effective fix for this – see 'Exceptions to the LCR rule' below.

Here are some advantages:

+ Clear and defined panoramic positioning of elements
+ Easier to mix when you only have 3 positions

Exceptions to the LCR rule:

1. Drum overheads – I usually pan these 50% L and 50% R, but this is based on the actual mic positions.

2. Delays and reverbs panned 50% L and 50% R enable more clarity with the effect because they tend not to mask other elements panned hard L and R. An exception to this rule can be the panning of mono reverbs to the same pan position as a kick or snare to add sustain.

3. Single source elements which are panned hard left or right can have a very

Amos Clarke

short (1ms to 10ms) delay panned to the opposite 50% pan position. This provides a real sense of space to the element without a noticeable delay due to the Haas Effect. See below how to do this.

Do It:

1. Using a unique element in your mix that only occurs in one pan position such as an electric guitar arpeggio or keyboard line, pan this element hard left.

2. Set up a stereo effects buss and insert a delay plugin. Create a send from your original track to this effects buss. Set the delay to between 1ms - 10ms and ensure all ping-pong and repeat settings are turned off. Pan this effect buss to 50% right.

3. Play your track in solo and slowly raise the level of the FX send and you will notice a subtle creation of space. This effect creates a real world scenario where both ears are hearing the sound source, with a slight delay to opposing ear.

Amos Clarke

25

Macro-EQ

Use a powerful, yet simple method to quickly EQ your entire mix

This technique goes hand-in-hand with the 'macro-compression' technique and is outlined in my other book, 'Macro-mixing for the Small Recording Studio' (available on Amazon.com). It involves applying EQ treatment to groups of similar elements BEFORE EQing individual elements.

Advantages for using this technique:

+ It's a quick, simple, and effective way to apply EQ to lots of elements simultaneously.
+ It yields more natural sounding mixes because there is simply less EQ processing going on in the mix.
+ There is less CPU hog on your computer.

Do It:

1. Set up 'group' busses in your session; one for drums and bass, one for instruments, one for backing vocals, one for ambient, low level instruments (add more as you see fit).

2. Route the appropriate tracks to each group so that all tracks except main vocals and lead guitar go to a group.

3. Apply a high quality EQ plugin to each of these groups.

4. With the EQ, start by applying high pass and low pass filtering to each group with the goal to allowing particular groups to dominate the high and low frequency regions.

Amos Clarke

26

Saturate It

Add definition and character to your mixes by adding in controlled low-level harmonic distortion

I love this technique because it's one you can have a load of fun with and there are almost infinite possibilities from subtle to face-melting, and everything in between. The technique involves adding harmonic distortion to existing tracks to add character, warmth, grit, analogue flavour, or whatever you want to call it. There are almost endless plugin options available, but let's start with a great free VST plugin that I use fairly regularly: Camelcrusher by Camelaudio, available at www.camelaudio.com.

Some advantages for using saturation are:

+ 'Thicken' the tone of an instrument
+ Accentuate particular frequency ranges of a track
+ Add gritty character to a sterile sounding track

Do It: Example using electric bass guitar

1. Add a saturation plugin to your bass track OR duplicate the track and apply the plugin to the duplicate (I do the second option when my plugin doesn't have a wet mix knob option).

2. Apply the desired amount of saturation to the bass to get a fuller, slightly grittier tone – but add it sparingly.

3. Listen to your effect with the entire mix going.

Amos Clarke

27

Mix Focus

Use automation to create and maintain focus in the mix

Maintaining 'focus' in the mix is an important part of creating a pro sounding production. In other words, we want to ensure that there's always something exciting happening for the listener continuously throughout the song. I like to think of it like a spotlight on my mix, which is always shining on something. For example, when the lead vocal is pausing between lines, we might have a short lead guitar line that 'fills the hole', or we accentuate a bass run, a backing vocal, a snare flam, or a keyboard part. The list goes on. It is a time-consuming process because of the automation process required and is as much an art as it is a science because it's your choice which elements you choose to accentuate. One important point is that these 'rides' are subtle and often only require a few dB of level adjustment to be effective. The fader adjustments are equally effective as increases and decreases. In other words, you can achieve clarity for one mix element simply by reducing the level of another for a short period – you don't have to keep turning everything up! Don't get this technique confused with 'riding the vocals', which is another similar technique used to create a consistent vocal delivery.

Do It:
There are two important ways to achieve focus in your mix:

1. The song is recorded and produced with mix focus in mind, so that there is always an interesting riff or lead part being played. This needs to be done at the pre-production part, prior to recording, but can also be added later. An example can be creating short lead guitar lines to 'fill the holes' between gaps in the lead vocal delivery in the choruses.

2. Automation is used in the mix to continuously adjust levels of different

Amos Clarke

elements so that there is always at least one element accentuated in the mix. What gets accentuated? Well, that's up to you.

Amos Clarke

28

Mud, Box and Honk

Focus on these three common problematic frequency regions to clear up your mixes

Excess frequencies can lead to an unnatural overall balance and listener discomfort and fatigue. While any dominant frequency region can be problematic in a recorded track, they can be exaggerated by multi-layering of same sounding instruments.

Three EQ regions that I commonly end up paying attention to in almost every mix:

1. Muddy region = 200 Hz to 300 Hz
2. Boxy region = 450 Hz to 550 Hz
3. Honky (harsh) region = 2 kHz to 3 kHz

Frequency ranges can dominate in a recording due to poor microphone choice/placement, poor room acoustics, incorrect amplifier settings, poor quality instruments, and poor recording converters (to name but a few). Cleaning up these areas of build-up in your mix will create clarity and definition.

Do It:

1. Get a rough balance for your song mix.

2. Listen carefully for clarity and definition in the mud, box and honk zones while listening to the entire mix. Compare your mix to a similar sounding reference song.

Amos Clarke

3. Identify the tracks or groups of instruments with offending frequencies and apply notching EQ with a parametric equaliser.

Amos Clarke

29

Vocal Clarity

Maintain lead vocal clarity in the mix by focusing on annunciation

This technique is a great way to improve the clarity of a lead vocal in the mix by improving the annunciation and adding 'air'. It involves a high frequency EQ boost while simultaneously applying a de-esser. This high frequency extension enables the vocals to have a forward 'in-your-face' character that stands out due to its slight dominance in the higher frequency range. With this technique, it's important to carefully balance the effect of the high frequency boost with the de-esser. The goal with the de-esser is to reduce the additional sibilance which results from the high frequency boost.

A note of caution:

+ Go easy with this technique and compare to your reference song to avoid over-doing it.
+ Use a good quality EQ plugin

Do It:

1. On your main vocal track, apply your best EQ plugin and a de-esser plugin. If you have a channel strip plugin with both these, ensure the processing order is EQ then de-esser.

2. EQ boost: using a broad (wide) bell curve, apply up to 10 dB of gain at around 10 kHz. The actual frequency and boost will depend on the vocal character and type of mic used.

3. De-esser: turn it on! Apply only enough de-essing to remove vocal sibilance while still maintaining the bright character created by the EQ boost.

Amos Clarke

4. As always, check this in the context of the entire mix and compare with your reference song.

30

Big Tune-Up

Drastically improve the quality of your mix by ensuring instruments and vocals are in tune

The perceived quality of your song production can be drastically affected by elements that are out of tune. Getting instruments in tune BEFORE recording solves much of the problem but you will often need to tweak and adjust during mixing. Lead vocals are usually the most obvious when out of tune and therefore require the most attention.

Common reasons instruments are out of tune:

+ Instruments not tuned before and during recording.
+ Intonation problems on stringed instruments (guitars).
+ Poor playing style on guitars
+ Wrong notes played

The biggest tuning adjustments will usually be for vocals and using a good quality tuning plugin (such as Melodyne) can solve most of the problems for both vocals and instruments.

Do It:

1. Use a high quality tuning plugin such as Melodyne.

2. Focus on single note elements such as lead vocals, lead guitar and keyboards, and bass.

3. Apply as little processing as is necessary to achieve correct pitch. Careful with over-processing on vocals as it can lead to an un-natural sound.

Amos Clarke

4. Listen to your adjustments in the context of the entire mix.

Amos Clarke

31

Parallel Mix Compression

Fatten up your mix by using this parallel compression technique

This is a simple and effective technique to quickly create a fuller, denser sounding mix. I use this technique on almost every mix I do. It is also known as 'New York Compression' and is a great alternative to simply applying downward compression to your mix. Downward compression can cause your mix to loose 'life' mainly because the compression reduces important transients from the mix and can upset the balance and frequency response. With parallel compression we are not affecting the dynamics in this way, but rather, adding to them. It involves using a high quality compressor plugin on the master buss. The goal is to heavily compress your mix then blend the effect with your original mix.

Do It:

1. When your mix is at an advanced stage, apply a high quality compressor to your master buss. You need a plugin with a 'wet' mix adjustment. I use PSP Vintage Warmer or PSP Oldtimer (available from www.pspaudioware.com).

2. Smash your mix with up to 10 – 15 dB gain reduction. Use a slow/medium attack (to allow drum transients through) and a fast release. Avoid 'pumping' and distortion. This should sound rather horrible at this stage.

3. The fun bit. Adjust the 'wet' mix so that you're mixing a small amount of this 'smashed' signal back into your mix. I usually start at around 15% and adjust to taste. You should achieve a subtly fuller sounding mix.

4. Once again, go easy with this technique. It's like chili powder: a little goes a long way!

Amos Clarke

32

Stop Trying So Hard

Quit the 'more-is-better' approach and start using subtle strategic techniques

If there's one thing that can completely wreak havoc in your mixes, it's simply over-doing it. I've been through this and it works something like this:

"In my struggle to get my mixes sounding professional I use as many techniques as I can, often resulting in over-processing. When I'm applying treatment to my mix, like compression or equalisation, I simply over-do it because I subconsciously work on the theory that if a little is good, then a lot must be better".

Do It:
Here are some simple approaches to avoiding the 'over-compensation' bug:

1. Practice using subtle adjustments with both EQ and compression. For example, if you're making a corrective boost to EQ, aim for no more than a 3 dB boost using a broad (wide) bell curve on your parametric EQ. Or if you're applying corrective compression levelling on track or buss, aim for a maximum of 3-4 dB gain reduction to keep the sound transparent.

2. Forget the 'more-is-better' heavy-handed approach and start crafting your mixes by using lots of subtle moves.

Amos Clarke

33

Mix Interest

Get creative with mix effects and processing by getting inspired by the 'best of' mixes by pro's in your chosen genre

Modern music is essentially and arrangement of similar parts in a particular sequence. The challenge is that when a part, call it a chorus or verse is played too often, it can get boring for the listener. Search the internet for the top ten songs for each year and listen carefully for creative inspiration. One of my favorite examples is Robbie Nevil, 'What's It To Ya'.

Do It: Creative tips:

1. Never play a musical section more than twice without an obvious new and interesting element. Example: third-time chorus has an additional guitar melody or the snare has a big reverb applied.

2. Treat your transitions. Transitions are the joining links between different musical sections such as intro and verse, verse and chorus, chorus and bridge, and so on. Example: the 4 – 8 bars at the end of a verse that lead into a chorus could have a chugging guitar with a volume swell.

3. Break-downs. These can be a verse or chorus with the main instrumentation stripped out. Breakdowns work well further into a song when the listener is already familiar with the part. The advantage is that the listener is familiar with the section.

Amos Clarke

34

Guitar Amp Sims

Enhance your tracks by using guitar amp simulators to layer in harmonic distortion

Here's another technique I love to use. It's very effective on almost any track, but I particularly like using it on lead vocals, snare and bass guitar. It simply requires you to add guitar amp simulator plugin on to your chosen track and then blend it back in with the original. For practical reasons, I almost always duplicate the audio track I want to effect and apply the guitar amp sim to this track while maintaining the original. This enables me to quickly and easily use the channel fader of the affected track to mix in the effect without having to access the plugin. The affect I usually aim for is a heavily compressed, slightly distorted character.

Do It: Example using lead vocal

1. Duplicate your lead vocal track and remove any processing on the track.

2. Add a guitar amp simulator plugin to the track and dial in some reasonably heavy compression and distortion. Add any other additional effects such as stereo spread or cabinet simulators.

3. Once you have the sound you're looking for, lower the volume of this affected track and mix in under your original vocal track to taste.

Amos Clarke

35

Width, Depth and Height

Create wide sounding, deep and full frequency sounding mixes using simple principles

This technique has a bit more real-estate provided due its importance as a topic.
The key to achieving width, depth and height in your mixes is firstly understanding the principles of width, depth, and height. Here goes:

Mix width

Relates mainly to panning positions but is affected by the location of frequency content in those elements. I like to achieve width by using extreme panning positions (left, right or centre). Secondly, ensure low frequencies (bass and kick) are in mono in the mix and do not extend into the stereo 'sides' of the mix, while high frequencies have stereo widening applied.

Do It:

1. Pan each track either hard left, hard right, or centre.

2. Pan low frequency elements to the centre.

3. Use a high pass filter to roll off the low frequencies for all mid-range instruments. For example, apply a HPF to electric guitars in the 125 Hz region.

4. Apply a multi-band stereo widener plugin on the master buss. Mono the bass in the mix by reducing the expansion to zero for below 120 Hz and widening the high frequencies above around 8 kHz. I use the multi-band

Amos Clarke

widener in Izotope Ozone to achieve this but there are other plugin options.

Mix depth

Relates to delay based ambient effects. Adding reverb can make an element sound further away from the listener, as opposed to a dry (unaffected) element sounding close. Imagine for a moment that you are creating a soundstage for your mix where you decide how close or far away an element will be in the mix. You can 'move' drums and backing vocals back behind the lead vocals by adding short reverbs. Ambient keyboard parts can sit comfortably in the 'back' of the mix by adding lots of reverb and lowering the level.

Do It:

1. Decide on which tracks/elements are to be close, near or far in the mix.

2. Apply short, medium or long reverbs to achieve this.

3. For elements up front in the mix, it's still a good idea to add a very short ambience to add a little space around it.

4. EQ your reverbs to that the low end and high ends are rolled off. This removes low boomy and high brittle characters from the reverb effect.

Mix height

Relates to a full and even dispersion of frequency content across the full frequency range of your mix. Combine instruments with complementing frequency ranges, rather than those with dominant frequencies that create peaks and troughs.

Do It:

This technique is outlined fully in my book 'Macro-mixing for the Small Recording Studio' – Available on Amazon here

Amos Clarke

1. Start by routing similar instruments to stereo group busses (drums, guitars and keyboards, backing vocals). Send lead vocals, lead guitar, and bass direct to the master buss.

2. Insert a good quality EQ plugin to each group buss and the separate vocal, lead guitar and bass tracks.

3. Before applying any EQ settings, decide on the approximate frequency range that each element/group of elements will inhabit in the mix.

4. Start EQing using high pass filters and low pass filters so that essentially, all you're doing is rolling off the top end or low end of each element/group of elements.

Amos Clarke

36
Add Some Air

Create lush high frequency sheen and give clarity to elements in the mix

This technique involves applying a gentle high frequency lift with a shelf EQ. It's a great way to bring out high frequency detail and works for most elements. Once again, don't overdo it. Adding HF detail to lots of elements in the mix creates masking and a harsh sounding mix due to, well, too much HF content overall.

I find this technique particularly effective on:

+ lead vocals
+ kick drum
+ Snare drum
+ drum overheads
+ Acoustic guitar

Do It:

1. First up, decide on which elements/groups in the mix will dominate the high frequency region in the mix and apply the HF lift to only those elements – I select three maximum (drum overheads, acoustic guitar, and lead vocals)

2. Using a good quality EQ, select a 'high shelf' setting centred around 10 – 15 kHz. I find the quality of EQ and the element being applied to, has an effect on the frequency selection here.

3. Start with a 3 dB boost and listen to the element in context of the entire mix.

Amos Clarke

37

Filter the Highs

Improve clarity of sonic space in the upper frequencies of your mix by reducing high frequencies

This technique involves rolling off (reducing) the high frequency range of selected single or group elements to create clarity for others. If all the instruments in a mix have lots of high frequency content, then masking and a loss of clarity results because different elements are competing for the high frequency real estate in your mix. I recommend an approach where you select which elements will occupy the high frequency range, and reduce the frequencies of other potentially competing elements.

Example:

In many rock mixes, I have the drums, lead vocals, and lead guitar occupying the upper frequency range. I limit most mixes to 2 – 3 high frequency elements playing at any one time. This means that I need to apply a gentle HPF to all other elements. For example, I often roll off electric guitars at around 5 – 6 kHz.

Do It:

1. Select the tracks or groups of instruments that will occupy the high frequency region of your mix, from around 5 kHz upwards. If required, create a gentle high frequency lift using a shelving filter on a good quality EQ.

2. For all other single track and groups of tracks, apply a gentle roll off using a high shelf filter.

Amos Clarke

38

RMS/Peak Compression

Hone your compression skills by understanding compression detection algorithms

Understanding this principle can make a huge difference in helping you select the best style of compression for the job. Compressors commonly have a peak or RMS detection circuit/algorithm which affects the way the compression works. Some are switchable (like Izotope Alloy) and some a set detection mode. In 'peak' detection mode, the compressor applies compression to the signal based on any part of the signal exceeding the threshold. In 'RMS' mode, the compressor looks at the average level and applies compression to any part of the average which exceeds the threshold. Peak detection is great for limiting and peak levelling. RMS detection tends to provide a gentler smoothing of the signal but lets the peaks through. Using two compressors in series can provide considerable dynamic control over a signal.

Do It: Example using an acoustic guitar track

1. Apply two compressors in series to your selected track. The first is a 'peak' compressor and the second, an 'RMS'.

2. Focus on adjusting the 'peak' compressor first (disable the 'RMS' for the moment). Adjust the gain reduction for around 3-4 dB gain reduction. Once set, move on to the 'RMS' compressor.

3. Adjust the 'RMS' compressor for around 3-4 dB gain reduction.

4. Overall, you should achieve a very solid and controlled character to your track.

Amos Clarke

39

Correction vs Character: Equalisation

Improve your application of EQ by understanding what you want to achieve

The key to applying any effect is knowing your goal first up before you start twiddling. Correct EQ and compression application is the cornerstone of any great mix. Here's how it works:

Equalisation for Correction:
Apply EQ to tracks and groups with the goal of reducing problematic/unwanted frequency zones. Examples:

1. Reducing a build-up of muddy frequencies in the 200-300 Hz with a parametric EQ.

2. Reducing sibilance from a lead vocal with a de-esser.

3. Rolling off the low frequencies of mid-range elements to create clarity in the mix

Equalisation for Character:
Apply EQ to tracks with the goal of creating colorful tonal adjustments to enable elements to sound more unique in the mix. Examples:

1. Sculpting a kick drum tone by applying a large bell curve reduction at 500 Hz and a small increase at 5 kHz.

Amos Clarke

2. Applying a 3 dB bell curve boost at 750 Hz to a left panned electric guitar while applying a corresponding cut at the same frequency to the right panned electric guitar.

Amos Clarke

40

Correction vs Character: Compression

Improve your application of compression by understanding what you want to achieve

The key to applying any effect is knowing your goal first up before you start twiddling. Correct compression and EQ application are the cornerstone of any great mix. This technique looks at approaching the application of compression based on what you want to achieve. Sounds simple, but it is effective. To put this into practice means that each time you insert a compressor plugin (or hardware) you ask yourself, "am I compressing for correction or character?" When you re-think your approach in this way, you will find you start selecting a particular compressor for the job. You may well find (as I do) that you add multiple compressors in series on a track to achieve correction and character. Or you may duplicate tracks and apply compression for correction on one track, and character compression on the other. There are lots of possibilities. Here's how it works:

Compression for Correction:
Apply compression to tracks and groups with the goal of levelling the dynamic range of the signal. Examples:

1. Limiting the peak levels of a vocal track to prevent clipping using a fast attack and slow release.

2. Evening out the dynamic range of a bass guitar track using a medium attack and release.

Amos Clarke

Compression for Character:
Apply compression to tracks with the goal of creating colorful tonal adjustments to enable elements to sound more unique in the mix. Examples:

1. Getting more snap from a snare drum using a medium attack (20 ms to let the initial transient through) and a medium release.

2. Getting a fatter, more 'glued' overall mix by applying parallel compression to the master buss.

Amos Clarke

41

Freaky Filters

Make unique sounds by mangling your audio

This technique presents a very effective way of turning rather ordinary everyday instruments into fresh and exciting sounds simply by applying a filter effect plugin to the track. The effects can be so unique as to render your original track un-recognizable – in a good way! My favourite plugins at the time of writing this is Camelspace by Camel Audio (www.camelaudio.com).

Examples:

+ Apply a 100% wet effect to a copy of an electric guitar track for short sections of your song, such as intro's or transitions.
+ Create a stereo render of one bar of your drums at a transition and apply a 100% wet effect.
+ Create a copy of your lead vocal track for the verses only and apply 100% wet effect for a unique vocal character.

Do It:

1. It's often useful to apply this effect to duplicate tracks, rather than the original as having the effect on its own track provides far more flexibility during mixing because the effect level can be controlled by a simple fader movement. You can also have only sections of clips you want the effect on, on your track.

2. Apply compression and EQ plugins after the effect for maximum tonal control. Compression allows levelling while EQ allows tone shaping, such as reducing unwanted resonances and low/high frequencies roll-offs.

Amos Clarke

42

Re-pitch it

Add thickness to lead elements such as vocals and guitar by making pitch adjustments

This is another very good technique for giving an element a unique character in the mix. It's also an 'old-school' technique but still a very effective one as it tends to add a thickness to the tonal character, providing a more distinction to that element. There are a number of variations on using this effect; from subtle to in-your-face, depending on your need. It does require a good quality plugin that allows pitch adjustments of very small increments. There are many plugin options available, with some specially designed for this application. Try Stillwell Audio's CMX Stereo Microshifter for a start.

Do It:

1. Apply your chosen pitch adjustment plugin to the original audio track, preferably after EQ and compression plugins as this provides a more controlled signal to the pitch plugin. Ensure your pitching plugin has a wet/dry control – if not, then you'll need to apply the plugin to a duplicate track.

2. Apply a +3 to +6 cents pitch increase and have this panned slightly to the left side.

3. Now apply a -3 to -6 cents pitch decrease and pan slightly to the left side.

4. Keeping both the re-pitched levels the same, reduce these so that they are mixed in at a low level 'under' the main vocal line. You should achieve a pleasant sense of thickening to the original track without it being obvious or over-bearing.

Amos Clarke

43

Chorus Character

Provide a gentle character enhancement to give elements distinction in the mix

This technique is just another way to provide a unique flavour to almost any element in the mix using a simple chorus plugin. There are a number of variations on this type of plugin, with some providing more advanced options such as stereo spread, or flanging and phasing options. For this application, we'll focus on the subtle approach where we use a small amount of the effect to bring an instrument/element to life. It tends to be more effective on tonal rather than transient (percussive) elements.

I've found this type of effect to be useful in two applications:

+ In very sparse mixes where due to the limited number of elements playing, I wanted each to demonstrate a more unique or special flavour.
+ In heavy, dense mixes where even after compression and EQ adjustments were made, I still wanted more definition for that element in the mix.

Do It: Example on electric bass guitar

1. Apply a good quality chorus plugin directly to your track OR create a send to a 'chorus' effect buss. Whichever method you choose, the goal here is to mix a low level effected signal back in under the original.

2. Ensure the settings have a slow cycle and shallow depth. Check that the plugin is not introducing any unwanted phasing by listening in mono to your soloed bass track.

3. Mix in to taste.

Amos Clarke

44

Limitation = Innovation

Extend your knowledge, explore new ways of mixing and boost your creativity

Ever been mixing and felt paralyzed by the shear amount of choice with plugins, leaving you unsure where to start and what to do first? Limitation is the opposite of excessive choice. When you limit your choice of tools (plugins) and set yourself an ambitious goal, you test your creativity, understanding and experience – how good are you really at mixing music?

I recently set myself the goal of doing the best full band multi-track recording and mixing production I could with a consumer quality two-channel recording interface, and a very limited set of standard plugins (four actually – they had to be either free or have come with the DAW software).

Here's what was tough:

1. Having only 2 channels available to record a full drum kit.

2. Getting the best out of one less-than-average compressor plugin, and the same for the one EQ plugin.

3. Battling with a sound quality that was marginal at best, due to the quality of microphone preamps and converters.

What was the outcome?

I learnt, intimately, the features and limitations of two plugins. I discovered a plugin that was far more powerful than I ever realised (having used it for

Amos Clarke

years prior to this). I felt tested and more confident with my skill level because I forced myself to rely mostly on my skills rather than gear.

Amos Clarke

45

Ping Pong Delays

Create fun and spatial dimension in your mix by using this creative delays

This technique involves using a simple delay plugin which is 'synced' to the tempo of your mix session. It's important that your song tempo is in time with the BPM of your DAW session for this to work successfully. You can add further character to this effect by applying EQ, harmonic saturation, reverb and more.

It can be a great way to add interest and depth to:

+ Lead vocals
+ Rhythm guitar
+ Drum loops
+ Keyboard rhythm and arpeggios

Do It:

1. Create an effect buss/track and insert a delay plugin. Ensure the plugin is set to 100% wet and no 'dry' signal is present. Ensure the delay is 'synced' with the BMP of your DAW session. Set the delay repeat to ¼ or ½ notes to start.

2. Create a send from the track you want to effect and adjust the send volume so that the effect is audible.

3. Adjust the pan position of your delay effect on the delay buss.

Amos Clarke

46
Phone It In

Add character and interest to a mix by creating this simple effect to any element

This is a very simple and effective technique and one that simply refuses to go out of fashion. It's often most effective when used sparingly: on a bar or two rather than throughout a complete song. Some call it a radio effect and others a phone effect, but whatever you want to call it, it seems to sit well with almost any instrument or vocal. In its basic form the technique simply requires limiting the bandwidth of the signal using a parametric EQ, however, adding limiting, compression, delays, chorusing, and other effects can add further dimension and character.

Do It:

1. Create a new empty track in your mix and label it 'phonefx'. Select short sections of audio clips from your other tracks and paste these clips to the 'phonefx' track. Ensure that any clips playing in the 'phonefx' track are not simultaneously playing in another track as this diminishes the effect. You could use phrases from the lead vocal and/or create stereo renders of your drum kit.

2. To your 'phonefx' track apply a parametric EQ plugin and roll off the low frequency at around 500 Hz, and the high frequency at around 2 kHz (feel free to vary these to suit).

3. Add a limiter or compressor plugin and set it to around 5 – 10 dB gain reduction.

4. Still on your 'phonefx' track, add a delay plugin with the delay set to 'sync'

Amos Clarke

with the tempo of your track.

5. Adjust the main fader level to taste and have fun.

Amos Clarke

47

Arrangement Transitions

Add a professional touch to your song arrangement by adding transitions between song sections

This technique involves taking any existing element of the song and using it to accentuate the transition between verses, choruses, solos, bridges and more. It provides a cue for the listener to let them know of the change to a new part of the song and adds interest to the production. A common technique is to render out short sections of your mix into one or two bar lengths, then locate these in the last bar or two before the next section. A duration of around one to two bars works very well with a slow fade-in over the duration of the clip. This creates a volume 'ramp' up which stops at the point of the next song section. Use care with this technique if you are using very melodic or strong chordal elements that can produce harmonic dissonance with the song. For example, using a rendered guitar arpeggio may clash with the bass line or main guitar chords at that point in the song.

Do It: Examples of transitions:

1. Open guitar strums or arpeggios with lots of delay or reverb, with a volume swell.

2. Stereo render of drum mix with 'telephone' effect and synced delay.

3. A stereo render of backing vocals reversed, with delay applied.

4. A simple automation increase of volume for a guitar, bass or drum lick.

5. A one bar stereo render of the drum mix put through a guitar amp simulator.

Amos Clarke

6. A short render of the entire song mix put through a guitar amp simulator.

7. A one beat section of any instrument of vocal looped and delayed.

This goes on and is limited only by your own creativity and imagination.

Amos Clarke

48

Satellite Monitoring

Get a different perspective on your mixes by listening away from the studio

This technique is a simple yet powerful way to check your mixes with 'different ears'. This is important because when you've listened to your mix 25 – 30 times or more, you can't help but lose perspective to some degree. As a mixing engineer, your focus – as it rightly should be – is on the science of the mix rather than the art. You're aiming for the technical: a well balanced mix; accurate tonality; distinction of instrumentation and so forth. It takes a well-trained and disciplined approach to listen for the art when you're in a technical environment. But as successful engineers, we must preserve the art, aura, and energy of the musical delivery. And a super-easy and effective way to do this successfully is this:

Leave the studio and listen somewhere else

It probably sounds too simple to be true, but I and many others have found this to be a very effective practice to carry out when you're near to completing your mix.

Do It:

1. Burn your mix to a CD or copy to a USB stick, preferably in .wav format or high quality mp3.

2. Listen in the car, listen on your home stereo, and listen through your mp3 player. Listen, listen, listen.

Amos Clarke

3. Lastly, keep a note book or other means of recording your thoughts about the mix. I guarantee you will come to appreciate your mixes in a different way.

Amos Clarke

49
Distort It

Add harmonic distortion to just about anything in your mix to create new sounds and accentuate existing

This technique involves applying a distortion plugin to any audio. You can use it very subtly to add warm, 'tubey' analogue flavours, or get heavy-handed and smash the daylight out of your audio – both options are fun. It's also a great way to add some grit to particular elements to 'dirty up' your sound. The possibilities are endless. What's more, there is an almost infinite cornucopia of plugins available; everything from guitar amp simulators, like Amplitube, to dedicated distortion plugins like Izotope's Trash. In addition to this, there are loads of free plugins that do the trick wonderfully – one of my favourites being Camel Audio's Camelcrusher.

Do It:

1. Create a new track and call it 'trash1' or 'drumtrash' – it really doesn't matter although it is useful to use separate tracks and label them appropriately to help you keep track of what you're doing – helpful in sessions with big track counts.

2. Insert your chosen distortion plugin and consider adding an EQ plugin after this in the chain to give maximum control of the tonal character.

3. Copy short sections of clips from any audio and paste them into your 'trash' track. It helps to add very short fade-ins and fade-outs for each audio clip to avoid clicking.

4. Check the audio levels of each clip in your 'trash' track (to avoid overloads and clipping) and adjust as necessary.

Amos Clarke

50

Compression Side-chain

Improve the function of your compressor by limiting pumping and incorrect detection

This technique will help you improve the quality of your compression by understanding how the waveform interacts with the compressor. This is an issue because compression action is triggered when a waveform peak exceeds the threshold. In many audio waveforms, low frequencies (that are often inaudible) have the most energy, exceeding the threshold and triggering the compressor into gain reduction. This is particularly useless if we are looking to compress peaks generally in the mid-range, which is often the case. Many compressors have a built in side-chain function, sometimes also labelled as 'HPF'. This setting allows you to select the frequency and below, that you want the compressor to ignore for the incoming signal.

Do It:

1. Select any track with predominantly mid-range material, like an acoustic guitar or vocal.

2. Insert a compressor plugin – ensure it has the high pass filter option outlined above.

3. Start with the HPF at a setting of around 125 Hz and adjust to taste. The goal is to get a smooth compression character that provides levelling which is not triggered by very low frequencies. To check this, disable or reduce the HPF to zero and listen to the difference.

Amos Clarke

51

Snare Thump

Get a fatter, meatier snare – period!

Some songs just need a fatter snare with more beef. If your snare wasn't recorded this way then here are two techniques to 'lard up' one of the most important components of any rock song. I use both techniques, but not usually together.

Do It: Technique A:

1. Many snares have a fat character around 215 Hz, so simply raise this frequency 3-5 dB using a reasonably (but not too) narrow bell filter on a parametric EQ.

2. Listen in the context of the mix and once again, careful not to over-do it.

3. A variation on this technique is to use a multi-band harmonic saturation plugin and treat only the 215 Hz region. This has the advantage of added harmonic distortion which can add a further lively and punchy character.

Do It: Technique B:

1. Accentuate the 75 - 100 Hz region using a noise triggering plugin which triggers a burst of noise off every snare hit.

2. If your plugin has a decay setting, adjust this so that the noise itself isn't audible – it should simply fatten the snare and not audible extend longer than the duration of the snare hit.

Amos Clarke

3. Use trial and error to find the best frequency to suit the snare in your mix and careful with the level.

Amos Clarke

52
Kick Thump

Sometimes your kick drum simply needs a good thump!

This technique will get you a thumping kick drum every time. There are two options here and I usually use one of them to provide a little enhancement.

Do It: Technique A

1. Simply use a bass enhancement plugin on the kick drum track and adjust to taste. I find that these plugins usually work equally well on both bass guitar and kick drum. It's that simple. WARNING: a little goes a long way and too much processing can cause clipping.

Suggested VST plugins: Voxengo LF Max Punch, Helian Third Bass by Fretted Synth (free), Waves MaxxBass.

Do It: Technique B

1. Insert a simple tone triggering plugin, such as the 'Sub-bass Synthesizer' available from MDA plugins (www.mda-vst.com) on the kick drum track.

2. Select a sine wave tone and select a frequency of 65 Hz. Adjust the threshold so that the sine wave tone is triggered every time the kick plays.

3. Lastly, tune the length (in ms) of the sine wave to match the exact duration of the kick drum. The sine wave tone should not be audible by itself but when blended with the original kick drum, should create a solid thump. Very pleasing!

Amos Clarke

Note: *For more options, consider a software plugin such as Drumagog from Wavemachinelabs. You can trigger sine waves and much more.*

53
Top & Tails

Create sparkly, clean starts and ends to your mixes

This technique is rather simple, but effective because it enables your mix to start and finish with clarity and precision and takes you another step closer to getting that pro sound. Cleaning up the tails almost always takes more work than the tops as many songs finish with a fade-out. This example will work on the basis that your song has a fade-out at the end.

Do It: Tops

1. Carefully check and trim the starts of ALL tracks in your session. Ensure you trim your clips just before the audio starts and avoid any unwanted noise. It's also important to add an ultra-short (in milliseconds) fade in to avoid clicks – most DAWs can do this.

2. Listen carefully with headphones on with the entire mix playing to ensure you have a clean start.

Do It: Tails

1. Check all clips and trim to the end position of the audio, adding a very short fade to the clip. Ensure you listen carefully as often quiet audio is not visible on a clip.

2. For audio clips with a slow decay, like the last strum of an acoustic guitar, carefully listen for clicks, knocks, breaths etc. These will require careful removal using software like Izotope RX or Stillwell Audio's Spectro – spectral editor.

Amos Clarke

54

Transient & Sustain

Get more control by manipulating waveforms

Controlling the transient and sustain elements of audio material allows micro level control over the dynamics of a waveform. Is it worth it? Absolutely, read on! The transient is the initial peak of the waveform and the sustain is the 'tail' part that follows. Simple! Newer technology allows us control both by using 'transient' plugins, however, the same results can be achieved using compression. The main reason to use this technique in your mixes is because manipulating the transient adds a tremendous amount of life and energy to your recordings by creating more vibrant sounding elements. Similarly, altering the sustain of audio material adds a fullness or thickness to the character. This means that you can use this technique very effectively with different combinations such as, only affecting the sustain, or only the transient, or both. Read on for some examples.

Examples:

+ Punchy snare – increase the peak transient to get the snare 'poking through' in a dense mix.

+ Bigger kick – increase apparent size of the kick by increasing the sustain portion of the waveform.

+ Accentuate guitar picking – if your acoustic guitar seems a little dull and lifeless, increasing the transient can add a little more snap and vibrancy to the character as an alternative to simply boosting high frequencies.

+ Accentuate a lead vocal – this works in a similar way to the previous example on acoustic guitar where the aim is to improve vocal intelligibility by

Amos Clarke

accentuating the consonants and beginning of sung words.

+ Smooth uneven picking on acoustic guitar – reduce the transient part of the waveform.

+ Short, snappy snare – increase the transient, while decreasing the sustain of the waveform (works a bit like a gate).

Do It: Using a transient design plugin

1. Select the track that you wish to manipulate and add a transient design plugin (see list below).

2. Simply adjust the transient or sustain parameter until you get the sound you're after. Most plugins of this type are very simple to use and only have a couple of knobs to twiddle!

Options: SPL Transient Designer, Stillwell Audio Transient Monster, Izotope Alloy

Amos Clarke

55

Consistent Hits

Get consistent kick and snare drum hits in your mix

This technique involves using a drum triggering plugin such as Drumagog, to trigger samples of your actual drums. Confused? Here's how it works. Inconsistent drumming leads to significant level and tonal differences between each drum hit and many times this is unacceptable in a typical rock or pop mix. Instead of replacing your drum hits with library samples, you can sample your best drum hit, load it into Drumagog and have it triggered by your actual drum track. Sometimes it works well to retain parts of the original drum track in the mix if your drummer is 'flamming' or playing ghost notes on the snare. In this instance you would create an additional track to place only the snare flams and ghost notes. You would need to remove these from the main snare track, which is the track you would be doing the triggering on.

Do It: Example using a snare drum hit

1. Using your actual snare drum track, find the best snare drum hit. Listen for level, tone, crack, and ensure there is no other noise such as cymbal bleed or tom resonances.

2. Render out this one-hit so that you have a separate audio file that you can import into your drum triggering plugin.

3. Apply the drum trigger plugin to your track and import your new snare sample and set up so that your existing snare track triggers your new sample.

4. Voila, you're done.

Amos Clarke

56

Vocal Creativity

Create amazing sounding vocals by applying a multitude of effects throughout the song

This is a great technique for creating interest to pop style vocals. The reason for using this technique is because it creates a continually changing 'landscape' of vocal flavours that maintain listener interest. This is particularly powerful if the song's arrangement is rather boring or the chord progression sounds a little basic because we are diverting the listener's focus onto the vocal. The application of any effects used can be either subtle or obvious – it's your call. However, when applying effects it does make production sense to be sensitive to the vocal's location in the song. In other words, it makes sense to concentrate your efforts in the chorus and bridge while pulling back a little in the other song sections. This process goes beyond simply adding a plugin effect and often includes looping sections, repeats, layering vocal renders and so on. There can be quite a bit of processing required but it can be well worth the effort, not to mention lots of fun!

Example of how I've used it in a mix

I wanted to really create some interesting in-your-face and subtle effects on the lead and backing vocals to a female vocalist on a pop mix. I started by getting the overall lead vocal sound I was looking for, which was very compressed with an enhanced top end clarity. Next, I identified locations in the mix that I would create effects. Firstly, I chose locations based on the song arrangement, like at transitions between verse/chorus/bridge etc, and at turnarounds. Secondly, I applied effects based on the lyrics where I'd simply listen for 'hooky' lines and affect these. Almost all effects were applied to a vocal phrase only, rather than entire sections.

Amos Clarke

Examples of Types of Effects

1. Telephone effect including variations using delays

2. Delays synced to song tempo

3. Crazy filtering – see my 'Freaky Filters' tip

4. Short sections of vocal rendered and reversed

5. Heavily limited and distorted

6. Guitar amp simulators

7. Re-pitching up and down in tone and semi tone intervals

Amos Clarke

Glossary

DAW
Digital Audio Workstation. In other words, this is the recording software used.

Element
Audio material within your mixing environment. It could be an instrument, vocal, drum or anything recorded.

EQ
Refers to the application of equalisation. In this book it mostly relates to using an equaliser plugin and includes high-pass and low-pass filters (HPF, LPF) although the reference in this book most often refers to a parametric equaliser.

Haas Delay
Otherwise known as the 'precedence effect', it is a psychoacoustic effect created when a delayed version of the original audio signal is so short it is perceived as being 'fused' with the original, rather than being a separate occurrence. It was discovered by Helmut Hass in 1949.

HPF
A High Pass Filter is a simple form of equalisation which controls the range of frequency allowed to 'pass through' above a given point. For example, if you set your HPF with a 'knee' or 'roll-off' frequency of 100 Hz, then frequencies below the knee will be attenuated, allowing those above to pass.

Pumping (compression)
An audible fluctuation in volume caused by a combination of attack and release settings in a compressor. An effect that is sometimes prized, but often unwanted.

Render
To create a mix (either mono or stereo) of selected elements in your mixing session, whereby a new audio file is created.

Amos Clarke

Roll-off

To 'roll off' is to create a reduction of either high or low frequencies above or below a 'roll-off' point using a high-pass filter (HPF) or low-pass filter (LPF). For example, applying a LPF at 5 kHz would mean a reduction of all frequencies above 5 kHz.

Transition

A point of change between two musical sections, such as between a verse and a chorus.

Amos Clarke

Thanks

Well, you got this far – well done! I want to offer you a very big thanks for reading this book. I sincerely hope you find value in it. This can act as a great reference to come back to as you try the different techniques and begin using them in your mixing workflow.

What did you think of this book? How did it help you? I first got the idea to write this book after a number of my studio clients began commenting on the number of 'tricks' I used during our mixing and production sessions. To me, I was simply operating in a way that was quite transparent to my mixing workflow. In other words, these small and complex routines were every-day fare that I didn't really see as anything different or special because I did them all the time. So, to cut a long story short, I got inspired to share the ideas with you. What I'd really like to know right now, is if you found them useful? Are there any tips you REALLY love? Are there any you can't stand? What works best? What are your 'go-to' tips you can't live without? There are a whole bunch of them that I can't imagine not using.

So please, let me know what you think. I would really appreciate it if you could leave me a brief review on Amazon with your honest comments and feedback. It's important because it helps me improve the quality of this book and future books.

What did you think of this book?

Please leave a review on Amazon

Sincerely

Amos Clarke

Amos Clarke

Other Books by Amos Clarke

Macro-Mixing for the Small Recording Studio:

Produce better mixes, faster than ever using simple techniques that actually work

Macro-Mixing For The Small Recording Studio is intended for beginner and intermediate mixing engineers who want to find new ways to massively improve their workflow and the quality of their studio mixes. The book is packed with techniques, examples, guides, and tips to help you create a 'breakthrough' with your mixing. The author includes anecdotes from his own experience working with bands and working on mixing projects.

Available on Amazon.com

About The Author

Amos Clarke has been working as a recording and mix engineer, songwriter and producer for well over 10 years. He's worked extensively in live sound and as a bass player and vocalist in working bands that have gigged around the world. He's also a lecturer at Unitec Institute of Technology in Auckland, New Zealand where he's being lecturing at a tertiary level for over 15 years. He holds a diploma in audio engineering from SAE, a Graduate Diploma in Higher Education and currently runs sHOWpONY, a boutique recording and production studio in Auckland, New Zealand.

Get in touch with Amos Clarke:

Email - macromixing@outlook.com

Amos Clarke

Made in the USA
San Bernardino, CA
30 July 2019